DISCARD

King Henry the Ape

Animal Jokes

Compiled by Charles Keller

Illustrated by Edward Frascino

 PIPPIN PRESS
New York
1989

For Nicole and Leigh

Library of Congress Cataloging-in-Publication Data

Keller, Charles.
  King Henry the Ape; animal jokes / compiled by Charles Keller :
illustrated by Edward Frascino.
      p.   cm.

  Summary: A collection of jokes about animals, such as
"What do you call a pig's laundry? Hogwash."
ISBN 0-945912-08-0   :
  1. Animals—Humor.   2. Jokes.   3. Wit and humor, Juvenile.
4. Riddles, Juvenile.   [1. Animals—Wit and humor.   2. Jokes.]
I. Frascino, Edward, ill. II. Title.
PN6231.A5K38   1989
818'.5402—dc20   89-8497
                                                                      CIP
                                                                       AC

Published by Pippin Press, 229 East 85th Street,
Gracie Station Box #92, New York, N.Y. 10028

Printed in the United States of America   .J

What's hairy, ruled England and eats bananas?
King Henry the Ape.

What time is it when an elephant sits on your fence?
Time to buy a new one.

What card game do pigs like best?
Porker.

How do you keep a skunk from smelling?
Hold its nose.

What do you get when an elephant squirts water through its trunk?
A jumbo jet.

Who tells long, boring stories about the forest?
Smokey the bore.

What games do hens play with their chicks?
Peck-a-boo.

What's a snake's favorite subject?
Hiss-tory.

How do you make an elephant laugh?
Tickle its ivories.

What did the mother owl say to the papa owl?
"Junior doesn't give a hoot about anything."

Why did the mother kangaroo scold her child?
For eating crackers in bed.

Why is a skunk poor?
It has only one scent.

How do you talk to a giraffe?
Raise your voice.

What's smarter than a horse that can count?
A spelling bee.

How do elephants talk to each other?
On 'elephones.

What do you call a rabbit with fleas?
Bugs Bunny.

Where do farmers leave their pigs when they come to town?
At porking meters.

Why was the duck giving orders on the train?
Because he was the con-duck-tor.

Why did the otter cross the road?
To get to the otter side.

What do you get when you cross an elephant with a fish?
Swimming trunks.

What do you get when you cross a turtle with a cow?
A turtle-necked jersey.

What animal do vampires like best?
A giraffe.

What's long and thin and goes, "Hith, hith?"
A snake with a lisp.

How do you tape record a monkey's voice?
With an ape recorder.

Why did the turkey cross the road?
To prove it wasn't chicken.

What do you call a crazy chicken?
A cuckoo cluck.

What frog was a famous Indian chief?
Sitting Bullfrog.

What do squirrels give their girl friends?
Forget-me-nuts.

Why shouldn't you bring a chicken to school?
It might use fowl language.

What did the monkey say when his sister had a baby?
"Well, I'll be a monkey's uncle."

What do you call a chicken that thinks it's Superman?
Cluck Kent.

Who caught flies and was the first treasurer of the United States?
Salamander Hamilton.

Why did the pig become an actor?
Because he was a big ham.

What are the hardest keys to turn?
Donkeys, monkeys and turkeys.

What do you call an airplane that carries rabbits?

A hareplane.

What two animals go everywhere you do?

Your calves.

What did the alligator say when he had a lot of homework?

"I'm swamped."

What's another name for a mountain goat?
A hill billy.

What do monkeys sing on Flag Day?
"The Star-Spangled Banana."

What do you call bears with back teeth?
Molar bears.

What pigs write to each other?
Pen pals.

What do you get from a forgetful cow?
Milk of amnesia.

What kind of dial should you never touch?
A crocodile.

What grows down?
Ducks and geese.

Why did the man collect 100 female pigs and 100 male deer?
He wanted a hundred sows and bucks.

Why do owls call at night?
Because the rates are cheaper.

What dance do horses do best?
The mustango.

Why do roosters never get rich?
Because they work for chicken feed.

What did the goat say when it ate the reel of film?
"The book was better."

Why don't anteaters get sick?
Because they are full of little anty bodies.

What's gray, has four legs and weighs two hundred pounds?
A fat mouse.

What do you call polar cows?
Eskimoos.

What do chickens say when they want to switch nests?
"Let's make an eggs-change."

When do rabbits have eight legs?
When there are two of them.

How do rattlesnakes keep in touch?
Poison to poison.

What did the porcupine say to the cactus plant?
"Hi, cutie."

Why are wolves like cards?
They come in packs.

What did the beaver say to the tree?
"It's been nice gnawing you."

Why did the girl call her pet fawn, "Ninety-nine cents"?
Because it wasn't big enough to be a buck.

What did the rich rabbit become when it grew up?
A million-hare.

What do you call an elephant who lives in Los Angeles?
An L.A. phant.

What do you call a feather storm?
A down pour.

What do you call a pig's laundry?
Hogwash.

How do you make poisonous snakes cry?
Take away their rattles.

Why did the rabbit cross the road?
To get to the hopping mall.

What goes, "croak, croak," when it's misty?
A frog horn.

How does a whale cry?
"Blubber, blubber."

How did the snake sign his letters?
Love and hisses.

What do pigs do when they play basketball?
They hog the ball.

Where do polar bears vote?
At the North Poll.

What did the duck say when it finished shopping?
"Just put it on my bill."

What do you get when you cross a jet plane and a kangaroo?
A plane that makes short hops.

What kind of story is about the three little pigs?
A pig tail.

What do ducks do when they fly upside down?
They quack up.

What does a pig use when he has a rash?
Oinkment.

Why did the dolphin cross the road?
To get to the other tide.

What steps should you take if a lion is chasing you?
Long, quick ones.

What cuts grass and gives milk?
A lawn moo-er.

Where do moles get married?
In the tunnel of love.

Why do mother kangaroos hate rainy days?
Because the children have to play inside.

What did the mother chimp say to the baby chimp?
"Stop monkeying around."

Which are the wettest animals?
Reindeer.

What do you call a squirrel's nest?
A nutcracker suite.

Where do you find a hippopotamus?
It depends on where you left it.

When do you get a busy signal when you call the zoo?
When the lion is busy.

What do you give an elk with heartburn?
Elk-o-seltzer.

What do Eskimos play polo with?
Polo bears.

What did the skunk say when the wind changed?
"It all comes back to me now."

What kind of bird can carry the most weight?
A crane.

What mystery books do owls read?
Hoot-dunits.

What did the sick chicken say?
"I think I'm getting people-pox."

Why does a bear sleep all winter?
Who's going to wake him up?

Why don't ducks go ice skating?
They're afraid the ice will quack.

What animal is on every legal document?
A seal.

What did the bear take on his sky-diving lesson?
A bear-a-chute.

How do chickens start a race?
From scratch.